Playing and Praying with God: Guided Meditations for Children

Rita A. Brink, O.S.B.

PAULIST PRESS
New York / Mahwah, N.J.

Dedication

*This book of prayers
is dedicated to the many people
seeking a deeper appreciation
and understanding of their
relationship with the Divine,
especially my family,
religious community
and the numerous children
who have provided me the opportunity for prayer.*

Cover and interior illustrations by Sister Emmanuel Pieper, O.S.B.

Copyright © 1996 by St. Walburg Monastery

All rights reserved. No part of this book may be reproduced or transmitted in any form or by any means, electronic or mechanical, including photocopying, recording or by any information storage and retrieval system without permission in writing from the Publisher.

Library of Congress Cataloging-in-Publication Data

Brink, Rita A.
    Playing and praying with God : guided meditations for children / by Rita A. Brink.
      p. cm.
    ISBN 0-8091-3679-1 (alk. paper)
    1. Children—Prayer-books and devotions—English. 2. Catholic Church—Prayer-books and devotions—English. 3. Meditations. 4. Bible—Meditations. I. Title.
BX2198.B75 1996
242'.62—dc20   96-28991
                                                                                                     CIP
                                                                                                      AC

Published by Paulist Press
997 Macarthur Boulevard
Mahwah, New Jersey 07430

Printed and bound in the
United States of America

Contents

Acknowledgments	iv
Preface	1
Imagination and Prayer	3
Hints for Leaders of Prayer	4
Introducing Children to Guided Meditation	5
Opening and Closing Exercises	7

Playing and Praying with Jesus, God, and Mary

Jesus Feeds the People	11
Jesus, the Good Shepherd	15
Eyewitnesses	18
Running with Jesus	21
Jesus' Love and Forgiveness	25
In Praise of Creation	28
I Am God's Work of Art	31
The Potter's House	35
Dance of God	38
Precious in God's Eyes	42
Mary	45
Mary: An Ordinary Woman	49
Mary: No Ordinary Woman	53

Playing and Praying During Special Times and Seasons

Beginning a New School Year	59
Beginning a New School Year	62
Thanksgiving	64
Advent	67
Emmanuel, God with Us	71
Walk to Calvary	75
The Empty Tomb	81
Close of the School Year	85

Playing and Praying with Creation

Stewards of the Earth	91
The Air We Breathe	95
Soil	98
Gift of Creation: Water	101
Gift of Creation: Water	104

Acknowledgments

Thank you to the many people who have been instrumental in the completion of this book of prayers. Special thanks to my religious community for its support in providing me sufficient time and space to reflect and write, the many readers of the various drafts of these prayers, my proofreaders who have given countless hours, the children who, over the years, have called me and encouraged me to lead them in prayer, my colleagues, and my parents—my first religious educators—who instilled in me a love for God and the wonders of creation.

Preface

Some twenty years ago I was introduced to the prayer of centering. Shortly thereafter I experienced the prayer form called guided meditation. It has been these prayers of quiet that have opened for me the opportunity to develop a deeper sense of my relationship with the Divine.

My experience in quiet prayer has led me to an understanding of what many writers have been saying for years. It is in silence that we discover our ability to reflect, to get in touch with what we cannot verbalize. In silence we meet ourselves and find safety to deal with our pain, and we discover the power of our imagination which can lead us to meet our most sacred selves.

As a leader of prayer with children I have come to realize the depth of a child's ability to see within. During the years that I served as a full time classroom teacher and as a principal, children have taught me of their own need for quiet to develop their relationship with God.

Children seem naturally curious. They are free from the complications that we adults place on ourselves, thus blocking our own powers of wonderment and discovery. Having listened to children I began leading them in quiet reflection, using scripture passages and offering several questions to guide their reflection. I later began to introduce children to the prayer of guided meditation, offering them the opportunity to delve within at their own level of understanding. I was at first amazed at the results of praying with children, sometimes with as many as seven hundred at one time, attentive to the prayer at hand.

Over the years, as I have led children in prayer, it has been the prayers of guided meditation that children have remembered. It was the prayer of guided meditation that children would request when plans were in the making for days of prayer during the seasons of Advent and Lent.

Each guided meditation was preceded by an exercise of breathing, providing time to relax the mind and body, thus opening oneself for prayer. The meditation was followed by time for journaling, picture drawing and/or discussion, depending on the age of the child.

My experience with children at prayer and the encouragement I've received from colleagues and friends have prompted me to compile this book of prayers. The prayers vary in length and content. I encourage you, the leader of prayer, to play and pray with each prayer long enough to make the prayer your own, personalizing the prayer, changing it to fit your group, shortening it to accommodate the age of the children with whom you pray, and perhaps encouraging yourself to become a writer of guided meditations.

Prayer is that which is spoken from the heart. May your heart speak to you in such a way that you share your gift of prayer with others.

Imagination and Prayer

The gift of our imagination holds endless possibilities. The literature we read, the art and music we experience, the technology that makes communication possible, and the entertainment we enjoy, all speak to the power of our imagination.

The human mind, a most treasured gift, holds limitless opportunities for discovery. Guided meditation capitalizes on the power of the imagination, getting us in touch with the deeper parts of ourselves, alone and in our relationship with the Divine Creator.

Psychology tells us our imagination is an inner sense. It is an inner sense that takes us to places unknown, offers sights and sounds never before seen or heard, and hints at self-knowledge not yet explored.

Guided meditation is the calling on one's inner sense, thus enabling the discovery of new insights. Guided meditation is our call to listen to the heart and the mind, not forcing, not contriving images. It is our call to be open and attentive to the images and sounds of the Spirit.

The first step in guided meditation is the quieting down of the mind and body. By the use of a slow deliberate breathing exercise, we begin to relax, thus freeing our mind to be open to the workings of the Spirit. A slow reflective reading of the prayer, from the heart, by the leader of prayer, assists in creating an atmosphere of quiet wonder, thus providing the opportunity for an experience of the unknown.

Guided meditation can be a powerful tool for self-discovery. Children of all ages enter into guided meditation, thus opening themselves to prayer that offers, in a noisy world, the opportunity for reflective play, the heart of spirituality.

Hints for Leaders of Prayer

Those wishing to be leaders of guided meditations can do so by following a few simple suggestions.

As a beginner of guided meditation it is helpful to read and re-read the prayer several times prior to praying it with others. Being acquainted with the prayer is helpful to the leader in setting the tone for prayer.

Several readings of the prayer allow the leader to adapt the prayer to the particular group by using local references where appropriate, and by adjusting language that may be more particular to a local setting.

A slow reflective reading of the prayer will use appropriate pauses, thus creating time for participants to respond in openness to the images and sounds of the Spirit; slow reflective reading is essential.

The leader of prayer need only speak from the heart to lead others in an exercise of guided meditation. Good leaders are persons of prayer.

Introducing Children to Guided Meditation

Children of all ages are naturally curious. Their minds are constantly questioning, examining and creating possible outcomes to most situations. As students of curiosity, children are ready for guided meditation.

My experience says: introduce children to guided meditation by leading them in guided meditation.

Depending on the group—its size, age, and maturity—one may choose to begin guided meditation with children by first leading them in an exercise of slow deliberate breathing. This exercise can be done for short periods of time, two to five minutes, gradually increasing the time to about five to ten minutes. If this type of exercise is used, you may wish to end your time by saying a prayer or listening to a reading from scripture. A short reading from scripture is also appropriate midway through the time of quiet, which ends with a prayer by the leader or a prayer recited by the group. Soft meditative background music helps to establish a quiet setting for prayer.

Though the place for prayer is not what makes the prayer, it is important to establish a quiet, comfortable setting, free from distractions. This can be accomplished by having participants sit in an erect position, legs crossed or feet flat on the floor if they are in chairs, eyes closed, and hands resting in their laps.

Opening and Closing Exercises

Opening Exercise

To begin each meditation the following exercise will assist participants in relaxing, clearing their minds of the day's events or present distractions, allowing them to focus on the quiet, thus creating an atmosphere for centering. The length of time for this opening exercise will vary from group to group, or perhaps from day to day. The participants' familiarity with this type of prayer will also be a factor in determining the length of time spent in preparation for the meditation that will follow. The less familiar the group is with this kind of prayer the less/more time they should engage in the opening exercise. Knowing your group is the best barometer for establishing the length of time to engage in this exercise prior to beginning the guided meditation.

Invite the participants to sit up straight, place their backs against their chairs, position their feet flat on the floor, rest their hands in their lap, and close their eyes.

The leader then says to the participants:

As you sit quietly,
    pay attention to your breathing.

Breathe quietly, so only you can hear your breathing,
    breathe slow......breathe deep......
        breathe in......and breathe out......

    Feel the air as it enters your lungs......

        Feel the air as you exhale......

Breathe slow......breathe deep......
 breathe in......breathe out......
be aware of the air that enters your lungs......
 breathe out......as you exhale,
be aware of the air as it leaves your body......
 breathe in......breathe out......
 breathe slow......breathe deep......

Listen to the quiet as you continue to breathe......
 breathe slow......breathe deep......
 breathe in......breathe out......
Listen......
 it is in the quiet listening of the moment
 that you hear Jesus,
 it is in the quiet of the moment
 that you hear God speaking to you......
Breathe in......breathe out......breathe slow......breathe deep......

Closing Exercise

Depending on the age of the children, you may wish to give them time to journal, draw a picture, share their experience of prayer with others, or sit in quiet for a short time.

Playing and Praying with Jesus, God, and Mary

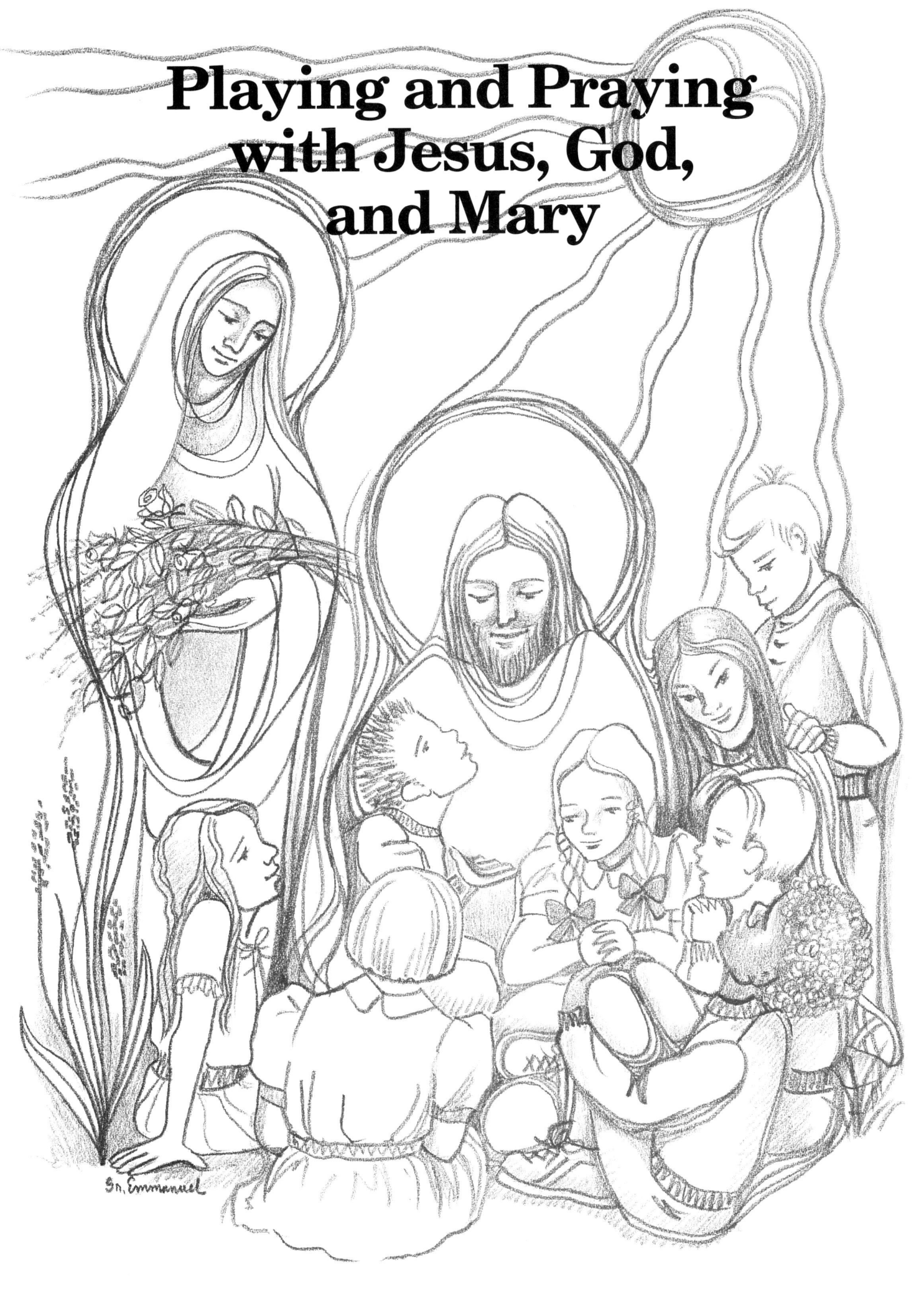

Jesus Feeds the People
(Influenced by Luke 9:11–17)

Begin this meditation with the opening exercise found on pages 7 and 8.

As you sit quietly knowing Jesus loves you,
    allow yourself to pretend you are an apostle of Jesus......

This morning you,
    Jesus, and some of the other apostles are going for a walk,
        you are headed for the park *(name a local park);*
            you have been walking for some time......
                as you approach the park
                      you are surprised to see so many others
                          in this same area......

You,
    Jesus,
        and the others look for a shady place to sit down......
            you see an area of shade nearby under a large oak tree......
            all of you walk over to sit in the shade,
                as you sit down, you slip off your sandals......
            Once everyone is seated and comfortable, you have lunch......
            it is almost noon time......

As you eat,
        the conversation is about several things you saw as you walked......
            after a while
                your conversation is about some of the
                    people you have seen
                        in the past couple of days......

    You and Peter had gone to Children's Hospital just yesterday
            to visit......
                you saw a little girl with both legs in casts,
                  a small boy hooked up to several tubes,
                      a baby with a temperature of 104 degrees,
                    and several children
                          who had had surgery......

After visiting with each child you offered a blessing......
　　you remember the smiles on the faces of each child
　　　　　　as you blessed them......

As you continue eating
　　you look around......
　　　　you notice that more people have gathered
　　　　　　in the same area of the park where you are sitting
　　　　　　　and they also are enjoying lunch......

After lunch everybody stretches out on the ground for a siesta......
　　it was a long and hot walk to the park......

After a lengthy time
　　Jesus wakes up feeling refreshed,
　　　　Jesus stands up and begins to visit with the people......

After a while Jesus begins talking to the crowd......
　　"I am happy to see that so many of you
　　　　have come to the park
　　　　　　to enjoy the sunshine and fresh air"......

Jesus then begins to tell stories and to teach the people......
　　everyone gets quiet and listens carefully......
Jesus tells the story about the farmer
　　and how he sowed the seed in the fields,
　　　　the story about the mustard seed,
　　　　　　the story about the farmer who went on a trip
　　　　　　　and asked the workers to watch
　　　　　　　　his land and money,
　　　　　　　　　and many other stories......

After many stories
　　and much teaching
　　　　Jesus comes back over under the oak tree to sit down......

Everybody who had been listening sits still,
　　the children begin playing......
　　　　some of the people come over to visit
　　　　　and thank Jesus for the stories
　　　　　　he has told them......

After a while one of the apostles, Andrew, says,
　　"Jesus, don't you think we should tell the people to start back home?
　　Many, like us, may have to walk a long way
　　　　and it is getting close to dinner time......
　　　　　They will be getting hungry soon"......

The people just keep sitting,
      waiting for more stories......
         "Instead of sending the people away,
            can't we just give them something to eat?" Jesus asked......

Think for a minute about how you felt when Jesus said,
      "Can't we just give them something to eat?"......

      All these people, and there is no food to give them......
         you say to yourself......
      Where does he think we can get food for this many people?......
         Andrew looked at Jesus and said......
            "We don't have any food......
               and there is no place close to get food."......

After Jesus thought for a minute, he said,
      "Tell the people to sit down"......

         After they all sat down Jesus stood up and said,
            "Take all the food you have
               and put it on the ground in front of you"......

      Some people had come to the park later in the day than others
         and had food with them for dinner......
            others had some food left from lunch......

Then Jesus asked the people to be quiet for a minute......
      When everyone got quiet, Jesus raised his hands,
         said a prayer, and blessed the food......

"Now," said Jesus,
      "share your food with those around you......
         make sure everybody gets some food to eat"......

      The people began to share the food they had
               with everyone around them......

      Several people brought sandwiches over to where you,
         Jesus, and the other apostles were sitting......

As you eat a sandwich
      you look around and are amazed
         at all the food that was being passed around......

Everyone ate and there was still food left over......
      everyone was having fun sharing food
         and tasting many different kinds of food......

After dinner the people wanted to hear more stories......
    Jesus said, "That is enough for one day......
        it's time that we all get ready and go home......

    Tomorrow is another day and we will all need some sleep
        to get our work done tomorrow......

So the people got ready and started to go home......
            ......

As you walk home
    you remembered some of the stories that Jesus told......

Sit quietly for a little while
    and let yourself remember
        several of those stories Jesus told the people......
            ......
              ......

As you remember the stories
    let yourself think about the fun people had
        as they shared their food......

    then thank Jesus for the stories and the blessings of the day......

When you are ready, open your eyes.

Close this meditation with one of the suggested exercises found on page 8.

Jesus, the Good Shepherd
(Influenced by John 10:11–15)

Begin this meditation with the opening exercise found on pages 7 and 8.

Knowing God loves us we sit quietly in God's presence......
    Today as we sit quietly we will think about shepherds......
        Shepherds are people who take care of sheep......
            Shepherds live in the fields and hills where sheep graze
              so they are near to watch over the sheep,
                  protecting them from harm......

Sheep are not very smart animals......
    They need someone to care for them......
        They need someone to protect them......

Remember the story about the night Jesus was born......
    Some of the first people to see Jesus were shepherds......
        They were nearby watching the sheep, protecting them......
           At night shepherds watch for wolves, coyotes,
                or a fox that may be out looking for food......

Shepherds have dogs called sheepdogs who help protect the sheep......
    When it hears or smells an animal coming near, a sheepdog barks;
        the shepherd wakes up and scares off the animal
                      to protect the sheep......

During the day,
    shepherds watch so none of the sheep wander off and get lost,
        or so that none of the sheep get stuck in a thorn bush
            or climb a rock so high
                that they will not be able to climb back down......

You and I, once in a while, are like sheep;
    we need someone to watch over us
        and protect us so we are not harmed......

    Jesus is our shepherd......
        He is constantly watching over us and protecting us......

                    Jesus protects us during the day while we are awake
                            and each night as we sleep......
                                    Jesus never leaves us......
                                            Jesus is our constant protector......

How do I know Jesus is with me protecting me?......
Think for a minute about a time you wanted to do something
        and you knew you shouldn't do it......
                or you were not sure you should do it......

        Do you remember hearing a voice inside you say,
        "You shouldn't."......

        The voice inside you is the voice of Jesus watching over you,
                it is the voice of Jesus protecting you......

Remember a time when friends asked you to come to a birthday party......
        or to the pool with them, or over to their house to play......

        You really wanted to go......
                so you asked your mom, and she said yes......

Remember the fun you had with your friends......
        While you were having fun,
                Jesus was right there with you having a good time......
                        He was watching over you and protecting you
                                as you were playing......

Sometimes we, like sheep,......
        are not very smart
                and we don't make good decisions......

        Once in a while our decision gets us into trouble......
                Remember what happens when a sheep is in trouble......
                The shepherd comes to help......

Think for a minute about a time in the past couple of days
        when you may have done something you should not have done......
                Tell yourself what you did......
                Do you remember hearing, at the time,
                        a voice inside saying,
                                "Don't do that,
                                        that is not a good idea"?......

As you think about that for a minute,
        say a prayer in your heart, asking Jesus to guide you
                and to help you to listen to his voice when he speaks to you......

Ask Jesus to help you to be a better listener......
......
......

Think about something you had fun doing in the past couple of days......
......
......

What was it you were doing?......
How did you feel as you were doing it?......

As you sit quietly, thank Jesus for the good time you had......
Remember to thank Jesus
for being with you while you were having fun......
......

As you think about Jesus as the Good Shepherd
watching over you and protecting you from harm......
once again thank Jesus for being with you......
......

As you sit quietly, talking with Jesus,
tell Jesus anything that is on your mind......
......
......

Now be quiet and listen to Jesus as he talks to you......
Listen carefully......
......
......

✠

When you are ready, open your eyes.

Close this meditation with one of the suggested exercises found on page 8.

Eyewitnesses
(Influenced by 2 Peter 1:17)

Begin this meditation with the opening exercise found on pages 7 and 8.

As you continue your breathing, relaxing in God's presence,
>> listen to the names of Jesus' apostles......

> Peter......Andrew......James......John......Bartholomew......
> Simon the Zealot......Philip......Thomas......Judas Iscariot......
> James, son of Alphaeus......Matthew......Thaddaeus

These men, twelve in number, saw many signs that Jesus worked......
> They heard the stories that Jesus told
>> as they followed him from town to town......

Each was an eyewitness to the happenings of the day......
>>> ......

As followers of Jesus, you and I are Jesus' apostles......
> We too are eyewitnesses of the signs of Jesus......
>> We are the tellers of Jesus' stories......
>>> ......
>>> ......

Jesus forgave people the wrongs they had done......
> We forgive people for the mistakes they make......
>> People forgive us when we make mistakes......

Jesus fed the people when they were hungry......
> We feed people when they are hungry......
>> We collect food to be shared with those who are without......

> Some of us help in soup kitchens to serve and clean
>> and have conversations with those who come to eat......

Jesus spent time with those who were sick......
> Jesus visited people when someone in their family died......

We visit our relatives, friends, or neighbors
        when they are not feeling well......
            Some of us visit people in nursing homes......
        We send get well cards
            or make phone calls to tell friends we hope they feel better......
We tell people we are sorry when someone dies......
        We celebrate Eucharist
            giving thanks
                for the life of the person now living with God......
                      ......

Think for a minute about someone you know who is ill,
            someone who is not feeling well......
In your heart, say a prayer asking God
        to comfort the person you are thinking about......
            Ask God to bring that person peace and grace......
                ......
                  ......

As followers of Jesus
        we see the way Jesus touches people's lives......
            We see the way we and others touch people's lives......

Like Peter, James, John, and Philip,
        we are eyewitnesses to the signs of Jesus,
            for we are eyewitnesses to the acts of kindness
                we do for one another......
                ......

Like Bartholomew, Andrew, Simon, and Judas,
        we know the stories of Jesus, and we are the storytellers!......

In our literature, in the games we play......
        in the plays we write, in the movies we see......
            in the poetry we read......
                in our day-to-day living, we meet the people of Jesus......
                we retell the stories Jesus told......

    The Little Prince, The Velveteen Rabbit......
        The Wizard of Oz, E.T.......

―――――――――――

Here substitute other titles, poems, plays, games appropriate for your group.

        Simple acts of kindness......
            the gentle touch of concern......
                shared celebrations......

The birth of a child......
    weddings......
        games played......tournaments won......

These are our stories......
    These are the stories Jesus tells through us!......

Like Thomas, James, Matthew,
        and Thaddaeus......

we are eyewitnesses to the love and gentle touch of Jesus......

    as speakers of the kind words shared with
        friends and neighbors......
    as those who care for the sick......
        burying the dead......
    as participants in the Eucharist......
        and the feeding of the poor......
          ......
          ......

Yes, we are eyewitnesses to the signs Jesus works;
    we are the doers and the tellers of Jesus' stories
        as we follow Jesus day by day......

Each of us is an eyewitness to the happenings of today......

Recite names of those present, if possible......

    you are eyewitnesses of the signs of Jesus......
        you are the storytellers of Jesus' stories......

What sign are you willing to share?......
    What story will your actions tell?......
        ......
        ......

When you are ready, open your eyes.

Close this meditation with one of the suggested exercises found on page 8.

Running with Jesus

Begin this meditation with the opening exercises found on pages 7 and 8.

As you become relaxed with your breathing......
    bend down and pretend you are putting on your gym shoes......

Today you are going to let your imagination
    turn you into a marathon runner......

Marathon runners spend a lot of time in training......
    They start off by running short distances......
        then gradually they add miles
            until they are ready for the distance of the race......
                ......

Training is hard......
    It takes a lot of endurance......
        It takes concentration......
            It takes focus, keeping your eye on the finish line......
                ......

To begin your training you set a schedule......
    You get up early each morning......
        dress......head outside to run......
            You find that some days it is easier to get up,
                to get dressed and head out for your run......

Every couple of weeks you add a few miles to your distance......
    Morning after morning......you run......
        some mornings wondering why you keep doing this......
            ......

One morning as you are running you meet up with another runner......
    The runner seems to be gliding along without any effort......
        perhaps the runner is just beginning to run......
            you've been running for about an hour......
                you're tired......you feel like stopping for a rest......

The two of you begin running side by side......
    after a time, the two of you begin to exchange conversation......

You find out your companion runs about twenty miles each day......
    "What keeps you running?" you ask......
        "The goal," comes the reply......
"The goal?"
    "Yes, the goal!"
"Do you ever feel like not running?"
    "Sure."
"Do you ever skip a day of training?"
    "Never."......

"Have you ever won a marathon?"......
    "You mean cross the finish line first?"

"Yes."......
    "No, I never have......
        I'll never cross the finish line before anybody else."......

"Why do you keep running?"
    "Because of my goal."

"What is your goal?"
    "My goal is to be the best I can be."......

    "I know I'll get tired and wonder what the heck......
        someday I may fall and get hurt......
            or take a route that seems harder
                and longer than another route......
        and I may have to climb hill after hill......
            I might even have to run through rain and snow......
                yet I'll keep running."......
                  ......

After you return home and shower......
        you sit for a while, you sit alone, in a comfortable chair......
        you think about your conversation......

You wonder what goal
    is so precious that you could keep it before you always:......
        straight A's in class......
            a good job when you grow up......
                a fancy car......
                    a new home......

Then you begin to remember
    some of the things Jesus said to his apostles and followers......
"Love God......

      Love your neighbor......
            Feed the hungry......
                  Clothe the naked......
                        Care for the sick......
        Help those in need......
             Comfort those who cry......

"Know that I am always with you......
All I teach you comes from God......

"This is my body, take and eat......
        This is my blood, take and drink......
              When you do this, remember me......

"Whatever you do for another you do for me."......
                            ......
                            ......

It seems so simple, you say to yourself......
    yet it is not simple at all......

To be a faithful follower of Jesus takes a lot of hard work......
    It takes endurance......
        It takes concentration......
            It takes focus......
                It takes keeping your eye on the finish line......
                      ......

Like the marathoner, it takes daily efforts......
    It takes constant practice......
        It involves falling down from time to time......
            It means climbing hills......
                It means running through rain and snow......

    It takes not giving up!......
        It means keeping your eye on the goal......
                ......
                  ......

As you sit for a while resting from your morning run......
    remember Jesus loves you every minute of every day......

    Jesus is with you to help you stay on your feet and keep running......
    In your heart, talk with Jesus......
        then listen to what Jesus is saying to you......
                      ......
                        ......

When you are ready, open your eyes.

Close this meditation with one of the suggested exercises found on page 8.

Jesus' Love and Forgiveness

Begin this meditation with the opening exercise found on pages 7 and 8.

As you continue your breathing,
    let your mind take you to your favorite place,
        your room......your backyard......your front porch......

    Once you are in your favorite place,
        sit quietly and think for a minute about Jesus......
            Remember, Jesus always loves you!......

When Jesus was on earth
    people knew that Jesus loved them
        because of the things he did for them......

    Today, you and I know that Jesus loves us......
        we know Jesus loves us because of the things
            Jesus does for us!......

Jesus gives us friends......
    friends at school......
        and friends in our neighborhood......

    Think for a minute about one of your friends......
        What are the things you do for your friend?......
        What does your friend do for you?......

A true friend will always help you in any way he or she can......
    A true friend helps you to act as you should......
        Jesus is a true friend to each of us......
            Jesus loves us so much that he died on the cross
                so we could one day be happy in heaven......

As you think about Jesus
    you know that Jesus spent his life doing things for others......

Jesus was a friend to many......
    Jesus taught people......
        He ate with friends,
            visited them,
                and had fun at weddings......
            Jesus took walks with friends and told them
                many stories......

Think for a minute about a time when Jesus helped another person......
    Remember some of the stories you know about Jesus
        that tell how he helped others......
            ....

Think about a time when you did something for another person......
    your parents, grandparents, a friend or a neighbor......

When you help others in any way you are acting as Jesus acted......

Remember that Jesus always loves you!......
Along with the love that Jesus gives you,
    Jesus forgives you the things you do
        that you wish you had never done......

    As you think about the things you do from time to time
        that you should not do, in your heart say "I am sorry"......

    for saying mean things about other people,......(I am sorry)
    for hitting someone,......(I am sorry)
    for knocking someone's books on the floor,......(I am sorry)
    for the time I laughed at someone who fell or dropped some books,......
                                            (I am sorry)
    for pushing or shoving another person,......(I am sorry)
    for not telling the truth so I would not get in trouble,......(I am sorry)
    for all the times I have done things that I should not do,......(I am sorry)

No matter what you do, Jesus' love is always present......
    Jesus always forgives you for the things you know you should not do......

Take a minute as you sit quietly by yourself and talk with Jesus.
    Tell Jesus anything you wish to say......
        things you are thankful for......
            things you are sorry for......

Then listen to what Jesus is saying to you......
                ......
                ......

Thank you, Jesus, for your love......
    for the good things you give me......

Thank you for forgiving me when I do things I know I should not do......
    Help me to become the person I am meant to be......
        Help me to be kind when I most want to play tricks
            or push someone I may not like......

    Help me to tell the truth
        even when it may seem better not to tell the truth......
        Be with me, Jesus, and watch over me......

Jesus, I know you love me......
        I know you always forgive me when I hurt myself
            or others......
                Jesus, I love you!......

Sit for a while knowing that Jesus' love is always with you......

When you are ready, open your eyes.

Close this meditation with one of the suggested exercises found on page 8.

In Praise of Creation

Begin this meditation with the opening exercise found on pages 7 and 8.

Today as you sit quietly in God's presence,
    place yourself in your backyard,
        under a shade tree at the park (name a local park),
            or sitting on the step by your front door......

As you sit,
    look around and see what there is to see......
        a rock......a leaf......perhaps an ant......
    maybe a small clump of dirt......

Whatever you find, look at it for awhile......
    Let your fingers and mind know its shape......
        Trace the object gently with your fingers......
            If the object is small, trace it in your mind......
                ......

What color is your object?......
    Does it have both dark and light shades of that same color?......
        Does it have different colors?......
            What kind of markings do you find on your object?......

After you look carefully at your object
    turn it over and look at the other side......
        What do you see on the other side?......
As you continue to look at your object......
    imagine the intricacy with which it was created......
        allow yourself to think about the love,
            care and attention your object was given
                as it was being created......
                ......

As you look at your object, observe its beauty......
            ......

As you sit alone in God's presence with your eyes still closed,
    look at yourself......your head......

>   your arms and fingers……
>   your legs……feet……toes……stomach……and shoulders……
>   look at everything about you……

What are you able to do because you have a head
>   with a brain tucked inside?……

>   What do your arms allow you to do?……
>   your fingers?……
>   How about your legs and feet?……

Think for a while about your heart……
>   and the blood it pumps through your body
>   every second of every day
>   and every second of every night……
>   ……

Imagine all those tiny blood cells running through your body……
>   they never stop to rest……
>   Your blood cells spend every minute
>   of every day carrying oxygen
>   and nourishment to all parts of your body
>   so you can breathe, and live,
>   and enjoy the wonders of God's
>   creation……

Think for a minute
>   about all you take for granted as you live each day……
>   as you take each breath……
>   make each movement with your body parts……

>   and then think about the love, the care,
>   and the attention that God gave
>   to the creation of who you are……

When God was creating the world,
>   God would stop from time to time
>   and look around at the shapes of things……
>   their color……
>   their texture,
>   and their beauty……

>   and God would look at what each object of creation could do,
>   then God would say……with great enjoyment,
>   **"This is good!"**……

The rock……
>   the leaf……

the ant or the clump of dirt......
whatever it was you looked at,
God looked at that same object and said,
"This is good!"......

As you look at yourself,
God is also looking at you......
your head......your arms......
your fingers and legs, and your heart......
and God is saying, **"This Is VERY Good!"**......
......

As you sit in the stillness and quiet of God's presence,
think about all that you are......
and all that you can do......
......

Thank God for the wonder of creation that you are......
......

Thank God for each day......
thank God for each object that you see and touch......
and thank God for each person you see......
......

Thank you, God,
for the gift of your presence......
......

Thank you, God,
for the gift of your Love......
......

Thank you, God, for making me who I am!......
......
......

When you are ready, open your eyes.

Close this meditation with one of the suggested exercises found on page 8.

I Am God's Work of Art

Begin this meditation with the opening exercises found on pages 7 and 8.

Sitting quietly in God's presence......
    Picture God as artist......
        ......

        Imagine for yourself how God looks
            when working in an art studio,
                ready to create a new work of art......
                    ......

As you look, is God standing with paintbrush in hand ready to paint?......

    Is God standing by a huge piece of marble,
        ready, with chisel and hammer, to chip away?......

    Is God near a table that is holding a clump of clay......
        hands ready to mold the clay into a new creation?......
            ......

What materials are waiting to be placed in the artist's hands?......
    As you look around the studio, look at all there is to see......

        Notice the various tools......
            the light in the room......
                the position of the artist......
                    Notice the look on the artist's face......
                        ......

Today in God's art studio
    you will watch as God creates a being that is you......
        As God works, pay attention to the love
            and the care with which God's hand makes
                every stroke of the brush......
                    or each blow of the chisel......
                        or the gentle touch on the clay......

Carefully......
    slowly......

     the new creation takes on its new-found form......
      Occasionally God steps back from the work
        and looks at the progress being made......
                ......

Looking at yourself as you are now......
  What do you see?......

    What would you change?......
     What would you add?......
       ......
        ......

After a while God goes back to work
    knowing what to keep......
     what to change......
      what to add......
       ......
        ......

With careful attention you are being shaped,
  and molded into the creation of who you are......

As you watch,
  notice the skillful hands of the artist......
    the care and love that makes each change,
     each addition to the work of art......
       ......

Notice the pleasure on the face of the artist as work continues......
  the gentle smile that comes with each brush stroke,
    each pounding of the hammer as it hits the chisel,
     each movement of the hands as the clay is molded......

How old is your work of art?......
  Is it six years old?......
    eight years old?......
     twelve years old?......
      somewhere in between......or older?......

Whatever age you are as you sit in God's presence,
  is the age of the object in the hands of the artist......
       ......
       ......

As you admire the patience of God's skillful hands at work......
  imagine yourself five years from now......

    ten years from now......
      What changes have taken place?......
       What has been added?......

As you imagine the changes and additions......
  think about the artist......
    Be attentive to the love and the care,
      the attention given to each move of the artist's hands......

Sit for a while with God, knowing that God
    is the Divine artist of all creation......
         ......
         ......

Remind yourself of the image of God as artist
  that you had as you began your prayer......

  Look around God's studio and remember everything you saw......
          ......

Look at yourself;
  the painting......
    the sculpture......
    the clay,
      being formed in God's hands......
       ......

You are God's work of art......
  Look at your shape, your color......
    the fine lines that form your person......
    Notice your smile......
      your walk......
        your height......
         ......
         ......

     All working to determine your personality,
      the uniqueness that makes you you......
         ......

In your heart give thanks for the wonder of your being......
  Are you as proud of yourself,
      as God is?

Give thanks to the God who has made you......
      ......

Give thanks for the care, the love,
    and the attention you receive from God
        who is always with you as you grow and change......

Give thanks for the gentle loving touch of the artist's hands......

    Give thanks for God's presence......
        a presence that never ends......

When you are ready, open your eyes.

Close this meditation with one of the suggested exercises found on page 8.

The Potter's House
(Influenced by Jeremiah 18:1–6)

Begin this meditation with the opening exercises found on pages 7 and 8.

As you sit relaxed, enjoying the quiet within, close your eyes......
    Allow yourself to visit the workshop of a potter......
        As you enter the shop look around......

    See the unmolded clay on the table......
        the various pieces of pottery that have been molded......
            the finished pieces with their colorful glaze and design......

Walk over to where the potter is working at the wheel......
    Pay attention to the potter's hands as the clay is worked......
        Notice the ease with which the clay is being pulled and stretched
            to create the desired form......

As you watch, the potter begins to talk with you......
    The potter tells you how the clay will be molded,
        by pulling and stretching, all the while creating the new form......

You continue watching......
    As the wheel turns,
        the clay begins to take on its shape......

    Pushing......
        pulling......
            and stretching,......
                the potter works the clay......

The clay,
    yielding to the guidance of the potter, moves with ease......
        The clay is pulled in, pushed out
            and stretched upward
                until the clay has found its new shape......
                      ......

Imagine for a while that you are the clay in the potter's hand......
    You feel the warmth of the potter's touch,

as the clay is kneaded, rolled and thrown on the wheel......
As the potter's hands surround you, the clay......
you become centered on the wheel......

As the hands that hold you,
the hands that surround you,
begin to pull and push and stretch,
you begin to take on a new form, a new shape......

As the potter's work continues,
be present to the gentle warm touch
that allows you to be shaped and formed into a new creation......

Be present to the pushing, pulling and stretching......
Be present to how you feel......

"Can I not do to you, as this potter has done?"......

In God's hands we are as clay in the hands of the potter......
being formed in God's image......
being formed in God's likeness;......

As the potter works the clay,
so God works in our lives
pushing and pulling and stretching,......
nudging and encouraging,
always with a gentle touch......

As the clay moves through the hands of the potter,
look at your shape.
Are you tall?
Do your sides move out and then come back in?......
Are you round?......
Describe for yourself the object
you are becoming......
......

As the potter gently brings the wheel to a stop,
you are lifted off the wheel and placed on the shelf......
Here you wait for the finishing touches,
the paint, the glaze, giving you your unique character......

"Can I not do to you, as this potter has done?"......

Think about your life with God......
Are you happy with who you are?......

Are there things you wish you would do differently?......
What will you change to be more like God?......

Spend some time talking with God......
　　　Let God know how you are feeling......
Tell God what makes you happy......
　　　Tell God what is bothering you......
Just sit quietly
　　　spending time with God......
　　　　　　　......
　　　　　　　......

When you are ready, open your eyes.

Close this meditation with one of the suggested exercises found on page 8.

Dance of God

Begin this meditation with the opening exercises found on pages 7 and 8.

As you continue your breathing,
    let your imagination turn you into a dancer......

You might choose to be a ballet dancer......
    an ice dancer......
        maybe a modern dancer......
            or perhaps you dance for fun,
                enjoying line dancing or just
                      moving to the music......

Whatever type of dancer you are,
    ballet, modern, ice dancer, or recreational dancer
                      you enjoy dancing!......
                      ......

You know that anyone who dances, either professionally
    or for the enjoyment of dancing,
        learns a sequence of steps and body movement......

As you begin to learn a new dance,
    step by step, movement by movement,
        your body is a little awkward......
    not knowing the smooth flow or the automatic rhythm of the dance......
                ......

To learn the new dance you practice, one step at a time......
    one movement over and over until it becomes automatic,
        until the steps and the movements become
                    as second nature......
                    ......

As you practice the footwork,
    the body movement of the dance becomes, little by little,
        more graceful, more automatic
            as the dance itself
                becomes more and more fun to perform,

>   more enjoyable......
>   more exciting......
>   ......

Your life with God is like the dance......
> as you—and I—learn more of the steps,
> > more of the movements
> > > that help us to live and to grow in God's love and grace
> > > > we discover more of the enjoyment
> > > > > of God's presence in us and among us......

Your life—our life—in God is a continual movement, a constant dance......
> It is the trying on of various behaviors......
> > It is the learning of skills for interacting with one another......

Your life—our life—in God is a time when we learn more and more
> of what it is that God has intended for us......

> It is a time when we learn more and more of who God is
> > and who we are in God......

> It is a time when we discover what it means to be chosen by God......
> > to be called friend by God......
> > > to be a child of God......
> > > > to be loved and forgiven by God......
> > > > > ......

Your life—our life—in God is truly a time of discovery......
> We discover right from wrong......
> > We discover prayer......
> > > We discover and come to understand
> > > > a little about God's grace, God's helping hand......

> We come to discover that kindness, gentleness,
> > caring, concern, sharing and cooperation
> > > are important steps in the dance
> > > > God wants us to dance......
> > > > > ......

> We come to discover that the graceful movements that make the dance
> > are all a part of our daily living......
> > > They are the discoveries we make
> > > > as we come to know ourselves and our God......

> They are the discoveries we make
> > as we come to know God's mercy......

God's forgiveness......God's love......
                                                            ......

Like the dancer
          as we practice the steps and the movement of God's dance
                    they become more automatic, more graceful, more natural......
                                                            ......

As you sit in God's presence as the ballet dancer,
          gracefully bending and twirling......
     as the ice dancer, gliding across the ice, leaping with precision......
          the modern dancer moving to the rhythm of the beat,
                    or the person enjoying an evening on the dance floor
          pay attention to the step and the movement of your body as you
                    respond to the automatic rhythm and tempo of the dance......
                                                            ......
                                                            ......

Then let yourself think about the steps and the movements
          of each day, as you live as a child of God......

Think about the steps you take,
          the movements that you make, letting yourself know
                    God is present within you......
                                        ......

Think about the way you greet others......
          the way you smile......
                    or help a neighbor or friend......
                              ......

Think about the way you play with others......
          work with others......
                    care for others......
                              ......

Think about your words of greeting......
          your response to another's question......
                    your conversation with friends......
                              ......

All of your actions......
     all of your words......
          make up the steps and the movements of the dance......

               What dance do you dance?......
               What is its rhythm?......

What is its harmony?......
......

What is the dance you will dance with God?......
......

Are the steps of your dance becoming second nature?......
......

Are you and God coming together as partners?......
......

Which movement, which step needs more practice?......
......

Sitting quietly in the presence of God,
   name for yourself the parts of your dance that seem right......
......

Name for yourself the movement or step
   you will pay attention to during the next couple of days......
......

When you are ready, open your eyes.

Close this meditation with one of the suggested exercises found on page 8.

Precious in God's Eyes
(Influenced by Isaiah 43:1, 4)

Begin this meditation with the opening exercise found on pages 7 and 8.

As you sit in the quiet of God's presence, close your eyes and allow yourself to think about the story of creation......
    God acting out of love......
        God creating a wonderful world
            to be shared with many living things......
                plants,
                      animals,
                          women and men......
                              girls and boys your own age......

In the beginning God created the earth and the sky......
    God created the plants and animals......
        and God created woman and man......

God created YOU!......
    YOU are the only YOU in the world......

Can you remember times when you've heard people say,
    "You look just like your mother......
        you look just like your father"......

    Have you ever heard people say, "You laugh like your brother......
        you laugh like your sister"?......

    You may have experienced someone calling you
        by your brother's name or your sister's name......
            yet YOU are the only YOU in the world......

It is probably true that you look like your mom, or your dad......
    and it may be true that when you laugh
        you sound just like your sister or your brother......
            people in the same family do look alike......
                and many times they sound alike......
                      yet YOU are the only YOU in the world......

The YOU that YOU are, is made in God's image......
    The YOU that YOU are, is the YOU that is precious in God's eyes......
        Every time God looks at you,
            which is every second of every day, God says......

    "I have called YOU by name,
        YOU are mine......

            YOU are precious in my eyes......
                and I love YOU!"......

God knows the YOU that YOU are......
    God knows every hair on your head......
        every freckle on your nose......
            God knows the sound of your laugh......
                your smile......your walk......

    God never confuses your looks, or your voice,
        or your laugh with anyone else's......
        God knows
            YOU are the only YOU in the World!......

In the quiet of your heart say three times to yourself,
    "I am the only ME in the world!
        I am precious in God's eyes,
            I know God loves ME!"......
                Repeat this twice in a whisper.
                      ......

Listen carefully and repeat to yourself what I say;
    Created in God's image, I am called by my name......
        ......

        Created in God's image, I am precious in God's eyes......
            ......

        Created in God's image, I am loved!......
            ......
            ......

When you are ready, open your eyes.

Close this meditation with one of the suggested exercises found on page 8.

Mary

Begin this meditation with the opening exercise found on pages 7 and 8.

Sitting in the quiet of God's presence,
    allow yourself to continue your slow, deep breathing......
                      ......

"Mary pondered all these things in her heart."......
        ......

Think for a while about Mary, the mother of Jesus......
        ......

Mary, a young girl of about fourteen years old
    is asked to make many choices......

        Will you be the mother of Jesus?......

            Joseph, an upright man, will be your husband......

                God will be the Father of your son, Jesus......

Mary accepted her call to be the mother of Jesus......

    She accepted the pain,
        she accepted the fun it would be, to be a mother,
                and a wife......

Mary enjoyed being with her family and with her neighbors......

    She enjoyed talking with the women of the small village
                where she lived......

Mary enjoyed the special gifts she had received from God......
    her gift of faith......
        her gift of being asked to be the mother of Jesus......
        and to be the wife of Joseph......

With all the special gifts Mary had received
        she must have experienced much confusion,
                      she must have had a million questions......

Who is this person with wings
        who is asking me to be God's mother?......

Is this a dream, or is this real?......

Do I know how to be a mother?
                I'm only fourteen years old......

Will I like Joseph?......

How old is Joseph?......
                What does he look like?......

Where will we live?......
                How will we pay our bills?......

What will Jesus be like?......
        Who will he look like?......
                What color will his hair be?......
                        ......

We, like Mary, have received many special gifts from God......
        We have the gift of faith......
                the gift of life......
                        We have our smile, and our personality......

Like Mary,
        we have within us the gift of the presence of God......
                Our gift is within us every minute of every day......
                        ......

Sometimes our days are hard......
        We are asked to do things we don't want to do......
                times when our mom or dad is sick, or a sister or brother......
                      or when a friend or a grandparent dies......
                          or when a friend hurts us
                              by what is said or done......

        When these things happen we are sad, we are confused and
                        we do not always know what to do......

        Like Mary, we sometimes have a million questions......
                        ......

Other days are fun and we feel happy……
    These are days when we get to do fun things like go on vacation,
        get a good grade on a project or an assignment……
            win a ball game……
                meet a new friend……
                      or stay up all night and watch movies……
                            ……

Mary went through some of these same experiences;
    she had fun days and days that were hard……
        ……
          ……

Mary's most treasured gift was her faith……
    Mary's gift of faith helped her and gave her strength
        to do the things God asked her to do……

Mary's gift of faith helped her to say yes
    to the angel who asked her to be God's mother……

Mary's gift of faith helped her through days that were not fun……
    and Mary's gift of faith
        let her enjoy being with her family, and her friends……
            ……

Mary's gift of faith let her enjoy being with the women of the village,
    and enjoy watching Jesus play
        and grow with the other children……
            ……

Like us, there were times when Mary had to ask God
    to give her the strength to face hard things……

    Like us, when Mary asked God for help, help was there……
            ……

Mary was blessed by God……

We are blessed by God……
    We, like Mary, have the gift of faith……
        We enjoy the gift of life
            and we know God will help us when we ask……

With God's help, we, like Mary, have the strength to say yes to God……
    We have the courage to say yes to hard things……
        and we can enjoy the fun parts of our life……
            ……

"Mary pondered all these things in her heart."......
......

Like Mary, allow yourself to think about the gifts you have received,
  your gift of faith......
    your gift of life......
      ......
      ......

Like Mary, think about the times you asked for God's help
  and God was present......
    ......

Now let yourself think about some of the hard things you have had to do......
  and know that God was present within, helping you......
    ......
    ......

Like Mary, ponder all these things in your heart......

When you are ready, open your eyes.

Close this meditation with one of the suggested exercises found on page 8.

Mary: An Ordinary Woman

Begin this meditation with the opening exercise found on pages 7 and 8.

As you continue your breathing,
    allow yourself to travel to the small town of Nazareth......

Nazareth is the town where you live......
    You live in the same neighborhood as Joseph and Mary......
        Jesus, their son, is the same age that you are......

When you arrive, in your imagination,
    in the town of Nazareth, look around......

What does the town look like?......
    Notice the houses......
        the yards......
            Notice the people you may see......

    Notice the children in the neighborhood......
        Who is there?......
            Are your friends outside today?......

What games do you and your friends play?......
        ......

As you walk farther down the street, you see Mary coming out of her house,
    Jesus is right behind her......

    "Hi Mary," you holler,
        "Hello there," comes the reply......

    "Are you children going to get together today?"
        "Probably."

"Good, I'll make a surprise for later."

"Thanks," you say as you run off with Jesus and the rest of the gang......
        ......

After what seemed like a short time......
        probably several hours,
                the gang comes back to Jesus' house
                      Mary has two plates of homemade cookies ready......
                                  ......

The cookies are great......
        the cold milk hits the spot......

"Thanks, Mary," the gang says in chorus......
        "You are welcome, I'm glad you are enjoying them......

Did you have fun outside together?"
        "Yes, we did!" several reply......

"Did everyone get along all right?"
        "We had a couple of disagreements."

"How did you work them out?"
        "We got together and decided what should happen."

"Good for you, that is the way to avoid further trouble."......
                              ......

One friend in the gang says,
        "Sometimes when we argue we get mad at each other
                and then it's no more fun to keep playing."......

"What do you think you should do when that happens?"
        "We don't know."
                "What do you think you should do?"

One person says,
        "I guess we should get together and talk about it,
                but when someone gets really mad
                        we argue and don't talk."

"Maybe that's when you should quit playing for a while and
        cool off before trying again."......

"Anybody want milk?"
        "No, thanks."......

The gang runs out and continues to play.
        Mary stands for a while at the window watching......
                            ......

When the game is over you head for home......
    As you walk along you think about the fun you had,
        the good cookies......
            the conversation......
                and Mary's invitation to come back again......

As you think about all of that
    you realize it is always fun to go to Jesus' house to play......
    the surprise that Mary has for you many times when you are there,
        the conversation,
           and the way Mary encourages you and your friends
                always to get along together......
                    ......

You remember the time all of you were playing ball
    and someone fell and skinned a knee......

    Mary cleaned up the knee,
        put salve and a bandage on it to keep dirt out......

You remember the time Mary took all of you to a movie,
    and then out for pizza......

You remember the times when you were smaller
    and you stayed at Mary's house
        because your mom and dad went out......

    You remember some of the stories she read to you......
                ......

You remember the things
    you have seen Mary doing that your mom does for you......

    cleaning the house......
        washing dishes......
           sweeping the floor......
                folding the laundry......
                  ......
              ......

As you sit quietly for a while
        think about Mary,
               and the many things she did for her family......
                      ......
                  ......

Think about your mother
      and all she does for you and your family……
                                     ……
                                     ……

As you sit quietly thinking about Mary and about your mother,
      say a prayer in your heart for all the things
            your mother does for you that you never think about……
                                                                ……

When you are ready, open your eyes.

Close this meditation with one of the suggested exercises found on page 8.

Mary: No Ordinary Woman
(Influenced by Luke 1:38)

Begin this meditation with the opening exercise found on pages 7 and 8.

As you sit in the quiet presence of God,
    let yourself think about Mary......
        ......

When Mary was asked to be the mother of God,
    she was a young girl......

    she was not married......
        she probably was not even going out much with the same boy......

If Mary were living today
    she would be doing some of the same things
        that girls who are fourteen years old are doing......
        ......

    Mary would be going to school......
        probably babysitting once in a while for a friend
            or for her neighbors......

    She would be going to movies,
        playing soccer, basketball, or volleyball......

    She would be going to dances,
        going out on dates,
            and helping around the house......
        ......

When Mary was a young girl she was asked to be God's mother......
    Mary, because she was filled with God's love,
        was able to say yes, I will be God's mother......
        ......

Because Mary was so young
    she didn't know all she was saying yes to......
        ......

Because Mary was filled with God's love
        she didn't need to know everything about being a mother
                to be able to say yes, I will be God's mother......
When you are filled with God's love
        it is easier to do what God asks,
                just as it was easy for Mary......
                        ......

Being a mother is not easy......
        Being asked to be the mother of Jesus
                at the age of fourteen was not easy......

Yet Mary, when asked, did say yes......

Mary said yes because she surrendered to God's love......

You are asked from time to time to do things that you say yes to,
        take out the garbage,
                clean up your room,
                        read a book and make a book report,
                              watch your brother or sister
                                    while mom runs to the store......
                                    ......

Some days you find it easy to say yes,
                and you do what you are asked......

Some days you are asked to do things and you grumble,
        you say OK,
                but then your mom or dad may have to ask you several times
                        before you do what you said OK to......
                        ......

Some days you do what you know is right to do......
        On other days you say to yourself,
                who will know if I do this or not......
                        and then you do things that you really should not do......
                                ......

One way we can help ourselves to be stronger
        and to do what we know is right is to think about Mary......

Mary can be for us a model of strength......
        a model of courage......
        a source of love......

When Mary was a young girl,
    she was filled with God's love......
  You are filled with God's love......
    and you know most times what is the right thing to do......

  Allow yourself to think about Mary
    and the strength and the courage she had
      when she said, "Yes, I will be the mother of Jesus,"......

  so you can grow in strength and courage
    to be able to say yes to what you know is right......

When Mary said, "Yes, God, I will do whatever you ask me to do,"
  she opened herself to God's love......

  When Mary said, "Yes, God,"
    she grew in strength and courage
      and was filled with God's love......

With Mary as your model,
  you can find the strength and the courage
    to be open to God's love
      and to be ready to do what God asks......
        ......

As Mary was filled with the love of God,
  each of us is filled with God's love......

  each time we say yes to God
    we open ourselves to God's love......
      ......

Sitting in the quiet presence of the Divine,
  think about Mary and her yes to be God's mother......

  and ask for the strength and courage to be open to God's love......
      ......
      ......

When you are ready, open your eyes.

Close this meditation with one of the suggested exercises found on page 8.

Playing and Praying During Special Times and Seasons

Playing and Praying During Special Times and Seasons

Beginning a New School Year

Begin this meditation with the opening exercise found on pages 7 and 8.

As you sit quietly, let yourself be alone......
    Now for the first time walk into your new classroom
        for this school year,
            stand in the doorway and look around......
                See the bright colors of the pictures
                      and posters hanging on the wall......
                          Look at the bulletin board......
                              What do you see?......

Notice the shiny floor......
    Look at the desks, not a speck of dust or dirt in sight......
        Notice the bookcases......
            As you look around
                everything looks new,
                    everything is bright and shiny.
                        The room is quiet, yet it holds
                            excitement......

Walk up and down the rows of desks......
    Touch them as you walk by......
        Stand in the middle of the room and let yourself look around......
            Tell yourself what you see......
                Tell yourself how it looks......

Bless the books, and the book cases......
    Bless the desks......
        the lights and fans......
            Say a prayer of blessing for your teacher......
                Bless your classmates
                    who will share this room with you this year......

Bless each person for their willingness to listen......
    to work hard......
        to study......

        Bless each person
             for the times each one will grumble and
               complain this year......
                   bless each person for the fun times
                       you will have with them......

Walk back to the doorway of your classroom......
    Look up and down the hall......
        Bless all the teachers and all the children
            you will see each day while you are in school......

Optional - - - - - - -

Think for a minute about the cooks,
       who will prepare your lunch each day
           and the ladies who will sell milk......
                Bless them, and ask God to watch over them......
     - - - - - - -

Bless the school secretary *(mention by name)*
    who answers the phone
        and takes care of all the papers you bring to the office......

Bless the librarian *(mention by name)*
    who will read to you and help you check out books......

Bless the people who clean the building, (mention by name)
    those who work each day to keep the building fresh and inviting......
Bless yourself and ask God for a good school year......

Think for a minute about others you may see this year
    while you are in school,
        the person who will deliver the mail......
            parents who will come to visit......
                (Add other persons particular to your building.)

    Be sure to say a prayer for each person
        asking God to watch over them and keep them safe......

As you stand in the doorway you hear footsteps......
    You look, and see someone coming down the hall......
        As the person gets closer you recognize him, it is Jesus!......

Jesus has come to visit you......
    Jesus has come to wish you a good year......
        Jesus is happy to see you and wants to listen to you
            as you tell him about your new school year......

What is your hope for this year?......
    Tell Jesus......

What is your fear about the new year?......
    Tell Jesus your fear, he is waiting to listen......
        As you tell Jesus your fear, he touches you......

Now Jesus wants to talk to you......
    Listen carefully to what Jesus is saying......
        "I can't wait," says Jesus,
            "to get to work in your new room......

"I'll be here every day with you.
    I'll be here with you when your work is easy......
I'll be here with you when your work is hard......
    I'll be with you when you are tired or crabby......
        when you are having a bad day......
            when you are happy
                and everything seems to be going right......

"You will never be alone......
    I will always be with you."......
            ......
            ......

As you sit quietly for a moment
    think about the things Jesus said to you.
        Remember, Jesus told you you would never be alone,
            he would always be with you......
                ......
                ......

When you are ready, open your eyes.

Close this meditation with one of the suggested exercises found on page 8.

Beginning a New School Year

Begin this meditation with the opening exercise found on pages 7 and 8.

Think about where you like to be when you want to be alone......
    your bedroom, your backyard,
        sitting in a rocking chair, on the porch......

    Where is it you like to be alone?
        Let your imagination take you there......
            when you are there, sit down and enjoy the quiet......

As you sit alone in your favorite place,
    Jesus comes along and sits next to you......
        After a while Jesus begins to talk to you......
            Jesus tells you three things he likes about you......
                Listen carefully to what Jesus is saying......
                      ......
                      ......

    Tell yourself what Jesus has just told you......
             ......
                ......

Jesus then asks you who some of your friends are......
    Tell Jesus the name of several of your friends......
        Think about each friend......
            What is it you like about each friend?......

Jesus begins to talk......
    "The things you like about your friends
        are the things that your friends and I like about you......

"You have many talents and gifts," says Jesus......
    Name for yourself the talents
        and the gifts you have......
        Tell yourself the things you like to do and are good at doing......

Your talents and gifts
> are part of what you bring to this new school year......

They are the things you will share
> with your teachers and your classmates......
> Tell yourself again what talents and gifts you have......

After a while Jesus says to you,
> "As you begin a new year at school
>> give thanks in your heart for who you are......
>>> give thanks for the talents and gifts
>>>> you bring to share with others......
>>> give thanks for what others will share with you"......

As you sit quietly in your favorite place,
> ask Jesus for the strength and the courage
>> to share your talents and gifts with your classmates
>>> and teachers......

>> Ask Jesus to help you share with others
>>> on days when you will be tired,
>>>> or maybe not feeling well,
>>>>> or a day when you just want to be alone......

In response Jesus says,
> "I will always be with you to help you do your best......
>> I will be with you to help you share your talents and gifts
>>> each day of the school year"......

As you sit alone for a moment think about your talents,
> about your gifts that you bring to share......
>> and know that Jesus is always with you......
>>> ......
>>> ......

When you are ready, open your eyes.

Close this meditation with one of the suggested exercises found on page 8.

Thanksgiving

Begin this meditation with the opening exercise found on pages 7 and 8.

Sitting in God's presence,
    continue your breathing,
        paying attention to the air as it enters your lungs......
            paying attention to the air as you exhale,
                quietly and slowly......

Listening to the sound of your breath......
    think about all the good things you have received from God......
        ......
        ......

Think about your family......
        Think about your mom and dad......
            Your brother/s or sister/s......

    Think about the house in which you live......
        the car or van you ride in with your family......
        your neighborhood......
            your friends and classmates......

    Think about your grandparents......
        aunts......uncles......cousins......your friends......
            ......

Think about each person you know......
    each object you and your family own......

    Think about your faith......
        the presence of Jesus Christ within you......

All you have is gift from God......
        ......

As you ready yourselves to celebrate Thanksgiving Day,
    sit quietly in God's presence giving thanks,

thanks for all that has been given you......
　　　　　　　　　　　　　　　　　　　......
　　　　　　　　　　　　　　　　　　　......

God, giver of all gifts......
　　　we give thanks for your presence in and among us......
　　　　　　for the gift of your Son, Jesus......
　　　　　　　　　for the gift of faith......

We thank you for all we have received......
　　　　　　　　　　　　　　　　　　　......

As we ready ourselves, O God......
　　　to celebrate in Thanksgiving......
　　　　　　we reflect upon the many gifts we have received......
　　　　　　　　　gifts that we often take for granted......
　　　　　　　　　　　　gifts not shared by all your people......

How Blessed are we, O God,
　　　to have a warm home in which to live......
　　　　　　a warm home that millions around the earth do not know......
　　　　　　　　　　　　　　　　　　　　　　　　　......

How Blessed are we, O God,
　　　to sit down to a meal of meat, potatoes, vegetables,
　　　　　　salad, milk, and dessert......

　　　a full meal that many of our sisters and brothers in Christ
　　　　　　know only when they visit a soup kitchen......
　　　　　　　　　　　　　　　　　　　......

How Blessed are we, O God,
　　　to have a change of clothes to wear......
　　　　　　clothes that are clean and fresh......
　　　　　　　　　while many have only the clothes on their backs......
　　　　　　　　　　　　　　　　　　　　　　　　　......

How Blessed are we, O God,
　　　to have cars and vans
　　　　　　and the means to take summer vacations......

　　　cars, vans, and money that others only dream about......
　　　　　　　　　　　　　　　　　　　　　　　　　......

How Blessed are we, O God,
　　　to recognize our faith, your presence in our lives......

        faith we share
                with all our brothers and sisters around the globe......
                                      ......

How Blessed are we, O God,
        we who celebrate your gifts to us in fullness and love......

            gifts you give to all people......
                ......

How Blessed are we, O God,
        who celebrate in fullness your presence in and among us......

            your presence that embraces the planet......
                your presence shared with all nations......

            your presence shared with the poor......
                        the stranger......
                            the outcast......
                                ......

HOW BLESSED ARE WE, O GOD,
    Remembering to give Thanks!

When you are ready, open your eyes.

Close this meditation with one of the suggested exercises found on page 8.

Advent

Begin this meditation with the opening exercise found on pages 7 and 8.

As you sit relaxed,
    let your mind wander to your favorite place at home,
        a favorite chair, your bedroom, the kitchen, etc.......
            Sit quietly and relax......
                Let your imagination run free......

Don't tell yourself what to think about......
    Be attentive and listen......
        Listen to what you might hear,
            listen to what your mind is saying......
                ......
              ......

In your imagination, fall asleep......
    As you sleep, you begin to dream......
        As you dream, you see before you people you know......

You see Abraham and Sarah......
    You see Moses and Miriam......
        You see Joseph wearing his coat of many colors......

Rebekah and Ruth are there......
    Isaiah and Jeremiah are present......
        Off to the right you see Jacob and David......
            David is playing his harp......

Looking around, you are amazed to see so many people you know......
    You wonder how David learned to play his harp......
        the music is soft and pleasing to the ear......

Walking around the room you look at all who are present......
    You smile at Moses......
        You wave to Abraham and Sarah......
            You give Isaiah a high five......

You catch Jeremiah's eye
        and the two of you exchange
                nods of the head......

You are present with so many people,
      yet it is as if no one sees you......
          You feel invisible to everyone......

As you continue to walk around,
      you begin to listen to some of the conversation......

You hear Moses telling Abraham
      about the long journey he just completed......
          You see Ruth and Esther talking......
              You see Isaiah talking to Jeremiah......
                  You walk closer to listen......
                  ......

You hear Isaiah saying,
      "Something wonderful is going to happen very soon."
          "What?" says Jeremiah,
              "I don't know for sure," says Isaiah,
                  "but you had better be ready"......
                      "How will I know?"
                          "You will know," says Isaiah......

The next thing you know you are listening to music......
      music that is very soft and pleasing to the ear......

    Listening to the music
          you become aware that you are the only person in the room......
            It doesn't matter that everybody has gone......
          You are alone,
              yet you sense the warmth of
                  someone close by......

Sitting alone for a while,
      you enjoy the quiet and the soft music......

In the quiet of your aloneness you hear someone whispering......
      "Hey kid,"......
          You listen......
              You hear it again......
                  "Hey kid, over here,"......

You look and see nothing......
      You listen......
          this time a little louder you hear......

"Hey kid,"......
        It sounds as if someone is right next to you......

Looking up you see someone standing next to you......
    You don't know who it is......
        It doesn't seem to matter......
            You say, "Hi!"......
                "Hi," comes the reply......

"Are you waiting for the Promised One?"......
    "Who?" you ask......
        "The Promised One,
            Emmanuel,
                God with Us!"......

"Who?" you repeat,......
    "The Promised One, Emmanuel, God with Us!" the voice replies......
        "Emmanuel, the one who makes all things new!......
            Emmanuel, the one who protects you......
                guides you......
                      and helps you through each day!......

"Emmanuel,
    God with You,
        the one everyone is waiting for is right here."......

"Where?" you ask......
    "Right here in your heart,
        the Promised One is always in your heart,
            sometimes you don't pay attention to the Promised One,
                yet the Promised One never leaves you."......
                      ......
                      ......

As you sit alone, think for a while about what you have just heard......
    "Emmanuel, God Is with Me!"......
        Keep repeating the line over and over to yourself......
            ......

Softly and slowly the leader repeats.
    Emmanuel, God with Me is always present!......
        ......

    Emmanuel, God with Me is always present!......
        ......

        Emmanuel, God with Me is always present!......

When you are ready, open your eyes.

Close this meditation with one of the suggested exercises found on page 8.

Emmanuel, God with Us
(Influenced by Matthew 1:23)

This meditation follows from the Advent meditation, using some of the same images.

Begin this meditation with the opening exercise found on pages 7 and 8.

As you continue your breathing,
      breathing slow, breathing deep......
           allow yourself to experience the quiet around you......
                  ......

Sitting alone in the quiet of God's presence,
      know you are never alone......
           God, who treasures your presence, is with you......
                  ......

Today as we sit in prayer we ready ourselves
      for the celebration of Christmas......
           the feast that celebrates the birth of Jesus......

"The Virgin, Mary, shall be with child
      and give birth to a son,
           and they shall call him Emmanuel,
                  'God with Us!'"
                  ......
                  ......
                  ......

Mary the mother of Jesus,
      carried Jesus in her womb for nine months
           providing warmth, nourishment, and love......

As people who believe in the person of Jesus
      we carry within us the presence of Jesus......
           we are nourished and loved by Jesus' presence......
                 we are filled with grace and blessings......

    we are treasured, we are loved......
            ......
             ......

Emmanuel, God with Us!......

  The Christmas stories tell of shepherds
    who came to see the newborn child......
      They tell of astrologers who came......
         ......

  I imagine there were people from the town of Bethlehem
    who came to see the newborn child......
      ......

Imagine for a while that you are one of the people
  who have come to see the newborn child......
    ......

What do you see?......
  ......

As you look around, who else has come?......
    ......

Do you see anyone whom you are surprised to see?......
    Who is missing that you would have expected to see?......
        ......

As you arrived to see the newborn child, what were your feelings?......
      ......

    After you were there a while did your feelings change?......
        ......

What will you say to Mary and Joseph?......
    ......

    What will you say to Jesus?......
      ......

As you sit for a while watching Jesus,
    say to yourself: Emmanuel, God with Me!
    Say it to yourself several times as you listen to each word......
            ......
             ......

The leader of prayer may wish to repeat several times in a whisper, Emmanuel, God with Me!

As you listen to the words over and over again in your heart
What does it mean to know God Is with You?......
......

Does it make a difference to know God Is with You?......
......
......

As you listened, what did you hear?......
What difference does it make
that God Is with You?......
......

In the quiet of your heart let the words speak to you......
......

Emmanuel, God with Us, is what we celebrate on the feast of Christmas......
Emmanuel, God with Us, is the meaning of Jesus' birth......
Emmanuel, God with Us, is our treasured gift......
......
......

Sitting in the quiet of God's presence, know that
Emmanuel, God with Us, is present in your heart......
......

Emmanuel, God with Us, treasures your presence......
......
......

After a short time, as leader of prayer, you may wish to pray this prayer, or one of your own.

Emmanuel, God with Us,
we thank you for your presence, and
for the birth of your son, Jesus.

Emmanuel, God with Us,
we thank you for your grace and your many blessings.

Emmanuel, God with Us, we thank you for your love, and
for each other......

May we, your chosen people,
    celebrate the feast of Christmas, the birth of your son, Jesus
    in a way pleasing to you……

        We ask this in Jesus' name. Amen……
                ……

When you are ready, open your eyes.

You may wish to close the prayer by singing an Advent or Christmas carol (e.g., O Come, O Come, Emmanuel, Silent Night, *or* The First Noel*).*

Walk to Calvary

Begin this meditation with the opening exercise found on pages 7 and 8.

Sitting in God's presence, continue your breathing......
    As you feel the air enter your lungs and leave as you exhale,
        take yourself for a walk......

Walk toward the town where Jesus lives and works......
    You've been there before, so you know the way......

    As you walk you come near a group of people......
        the people seem very solemn, very quiet......

The atmosphere lets you know something unusual is happening......
    ......

For a while you stay behind the other people
    so as not to interrupt the silence......
        You would like to know what this is all about......
            yet your sense tells you not to ask......
                you allow yourself to follow along in silence......

As you walk you see people you know......
        people from the town......
             Looking around, you see for yourself
                just what is happening......

Surrounded by soldiers......
    you see Jesus carrying a large cross
        a cross made from huge tree limbs......

Jesus is perspiring......
    Though Jesus is strong, it is obvious that the cross is heavy......
        You are surprised that no one is helping Jesus......

As Jesus continues to walk, he stumbles on a rock in the roadway......
    Jesus falls......
        The large beams of the cross
            fall across Jesus' shoulder cutting him......

　　　　　　　　The people gasp......
　　　　　　　　　　　Some begin to cry......
　　　　　　　　　　　　　　......

　　　　　　　　　　The soldiers begin beating Jesus with their big
　　　　　　　　　　whips......

Still no one tries to help......
　　　It's as if the people are paralyzed......
　　　　　　......

　　　No one is making a sound
　　　　　　except the soldiers who continue to beat Jesus......
　　　　　　　　　One soldier is yelling, "Get up......get up!"......

As Jesus tries to get back up
　　　you want to help, yet your body won't let you move......
　　　　　　like the others you are stuck in place......

As you stand there, you ask yourself, "Why don't I help?......
　　　Why do I just stand here?......
　　　　　　What keeps me from moving?"......
　　　　　　　　　......

Jesus finally manages to get up......
　　　It is with great courage that Jesus continues to walk......
　　　　　　Jesus looks very tired; Jesus looks worn out......
　　　　　　　　　......

As Jesus passes in front of where you are standing,
　　　you look down, hoping he does not recognize you......

　　　　　With head bowed,
　　　　　　　　your heart tells you that Jesus knows you and sees you......

As Jesus continues to walk
　　　with the heavy cross resting on his shoulder,
　　　　　the soldiers surround him......
　　　　　　　　With everyone else you continue walking in silence......
　　　　　　　　　　　......

You have a peculiar feeling,
　　　a feeling you've not experienced before......
　　　　　You are puzzled as to why no one
　　　　　　　　is helping Jesus carry the cross......
　　　　　　　　　　......

76

You do not feel free to help either......
        You think about how you are feeling......
        You wonder, what is going on?
                Why can't I help?......
                      ......
                      ......

A little while later, Jesus falls again,
    the crossbeam once again falling on Jesus' shoulders......
        The soldiers begin yelling......"Get up......get up!"......
        Jesus can hardly move......

The soldiers pull a man from the crowd to help Jesus......
    The man is reluctant to volunteer......
        The soldiers pull him,
            almost throwing him onto the road,
                making him help carry the cross......

You are frightened......
    yet you are relieved that the soldiers didn't pick you......
        You hope no one sees you......
        You want to leave......
            You want to get away from what is happening......

Yet, you can't leave......

    You don't want Jesus to see you......
        You don't want anyone you know to see you......
                ......

You wish you could disappear......
        ......
      ......
Yet you can't leave......

As you continue to walk, you fall farther behind,
    so no one knows you are there......
        You are puzzled by the experience......

You try to sort out what is happening within yourself......
    What are your feelings?
        Can you name your feelings?......
            ......
          ......

What are your thoughts?
> Tell them to yourself......
>> ......
>> ......

What is your prayer?
> Say it in your heart......
>> ......

With your feelings, with your thoughts and with your prayer,
> you continue to follow
>> as Jesus is made to keep moving along the road......

No one is talking......
> No one is leaving......
>> When Jesus falls, everyone gasps,
>>> almost in silence, so as not to be heard......

> Each time Jesus falls
>> the soldiers yell and beat Jesus
>>> with the whips they are carrying......
>>>> ......

After what seemed like forever, Jesus reaches the top of the hill......
> The soldiers take the cross from Jesus
>> and Jesus falls to the ground......

> The soldiers then pull Jesus' body,
>> placing his body on top of the cross he carried up the hill......

> They pull and stretch
>> until Jesus' arms stretch the length of the crossbeam......
>>> They place his feet together, one on top of the other......

Tying his arms and legs in place,
> they then hammer huge nails into his hands and feet......

The crowd is more silent than before......
> People are gasping and crying at the actions of the soldiers......
>>>> ......

No one leaves......
> The soldiers raise the cross,
>>> leaving Jesus to hang,
>>>>> leaving Jesus to die......
>>>>>> ......
>>>>>>> ......

Paralyzed by the day's events, you stand in place......
......

Hours later, Jesus cries out,
    then Jesus' head drops, and he dies......

For a while nothing happens.
    Finally a man from the crowd moves toward Jesus
        and begins to take Jesus down from the cross......

You move forward to help......
    ......

You help carry the body of Jesus to a nearby tomb......
    The body is prepared for burial and placed inside the tomb......

You sit down on the ground for a while
    remembering the journey you have just walked with Jesus......

    You remember the crowd you saw
        when you did not know what was happening......

    You remember the appearance of Jesus
        with the cross resting on his shoulder.....

    the treatment of the soldiers whenever Jesus fell......

    You remember not being able to reach out and help......

    You remember your feelings......
        your thoughts......
            your prayer......

    You remember the sound of the hammer
        as the soldier drove the nails into Jesus' hands and feet......

    You hear the silence throughout the whole day......
        the stillness as Jesus hung on the cross......

    the outcry of Jesus just before he died......

    You are aware of your feelings
        as you sit knowing Jesus has died and has been buried......

    As you sit in silence, let yourself recall the events of the day......
        and know in your heart that Jesus' love for you is the
            most precious gift you have......

Know that Jesus did all of this for love of you......
......

Jesus, you died for love of me.
    Keep me in your love and help me to know you more......
        Keep me safe, make me strong as you are strong......
           Fill me with your love
                and give me the courage to live for you......

When you are ready, open your eyes.

Close this meditation with one of the suggested exercises found on page 8.

The Empty Tomb

This meditation follows from the Walk to Calvary meditation, using some of the same images and events.

Begin this meditation with the opening exercise found on pages 7 and 8.

As you continue your breathing......
    breathing slow......breathing deep......
        relax in the quiet presence of God......

Resting in God's presence,
    allow your mind to recall the events of a few days ago......

    the day you followed Jesus, as he carried his cross up the hill......

        that day you hoped no one saw you......

You remember not being able to help Jesus carry his cross......

You remember the sound of the nails as they were hammered
        into the hands and feet of Jesus......

    and you remember helping to place Jesus in the grave......
        ......

Sitting with these events
    your mind begins to fill with all kinds of thoughts......

You remember that after the body of Jesus was placed in the grave
    and the stone was put in place,
        soldiers stood guard,
            not letting anyone close to the grave......
        ......

Remembering all this,
    you decide to go back to where Jesus was buried
        and see what is happening......

It is early on a Sunday morning......
    just a few days since Jesus was buried......
        As you walk toward the grave
            you see a woman running in the opposite direction......
    You think she looks familiar......
        yet you are not sure......

As you get closer to the grave you get a funny feeling......
        Something is wrong......
            What could be the matter?......
                The soldiers are gone......
        The grave has been opened......

You run the last few yards to see what is happening......
        looking inside you see nothing......
            just the empty grave......
You wonder what has happened......
        Did the soldiers take the body of Jesus somewhere else?......
                                        ......

Not knowing what to do,
    you just stand for a while,
        then you start back home......

On the way you pass several others running toward the grave......
    You think you recognize them,
        They look like people you saw
            standing at the foot of the cross a few days ago......
                              ......

On your way out of the cemetery
    a man sitting under a tree calls you by name and greets you......

    You wave and keep going......
        You wonder who he was......
            ......

When you get home you tell your parents what you saw......

    After a little while you turn on the TV
    You hear a news headline......

This is *(use the name of a local newscaster)* _____
    reporting live from *(name a local cemetery, and town)* _____
        It seems that the grave of Jesus has been opened
            and the body is nowhere to be found......
                ......

Several townspeople who are here
    say a man sitting over under a tree called them by name,
        yet no one seems to know the man......
                    ......

Later in the day while watching TV another news report is given......
    Good afternoon this is *(name the newscaster by name)* _____
        reporting live once again from *(name cemetery)* _____

We have further information on the happenings of this morning......

    The man they call Jesus has risen......
        Yes, after being in the grave since late Friday afternoon
            Jesus has risen from the dead......

Our research has led us
    to information about this happening......

It is recorded in Luke's gospel......
    in Jesus' own words, he says......

"I must endure many sufferings,
    be rejected by the elders, the high priest, and the scribes,
        I will be put to death,
            and be raised up on the third day."......
                        ......
                        ......

Perhaps if we had known more about this man Jesus,
    we would have been able
        to understand the happenings of the past few days......
                    ......

Perhaps if we had known more about this man called Jesus,
    we would have known what was going to happen this morning......
                        ......

As it is we are all still learning......
    We have much to learn about this man they call Jesus......
        Today, though, we have much for which to be thankful......
            For Jesus is with us......
                Jesus has risen and is with us......

This is *(name newscaster)* _____
    signing off for now,

    We will keep you posted on the coming events......
        in the meantime
        Let Us Rejoice That Jesus Has Risen!......

With the TV turned off
    you sit in the quiet, thinking about all that you have heard and seen......

You remember the events of a few days ago......
                  ......

    the events of this morning when you went to the cemetery
        and found the empty grave......
              ......

    You wonder about the man under the tree who knew your name......
        Who was he?......
            How did he know your name?......
                ......

    You remember the information about Jesus
        and his telling us himself
            that he would die and come back to life......
                ......
                  ......

As you think about all you have seen, heard
    and now know, you begin to say to yourself,

    Jesus is one special person......
        ......

        Jesus is one special person I need to know more about......
                ......

        Jesus is risen and is with me......
            ......
            ......

After a while you hear church bells ringing......
    You think you hear people singing......
        ......

When you are ready, open your eyes.

Leader may wish to begin singing in a soft voice The Celtic Alleluia, Jesus Christ Is Risen Today, Christ the Lord Is Risen Today, *or another Easter hymn, inviting all to sing along.*

Close of the School Year

This meditation uses some of the same images as the first meditation for Beginning a New School Year.

Begin this meditation with the opening exercise found on pages 7 and 8.

Sitting in God's presence, relax
    knowing God is present within......

Well, the day has finally arrived......
    Today is the last day of classes for a while......

You've worked hard......
    You have learned many new pieces of information......
        and you have seen a little better
            how various things work together......

You have experienced a few more intricate
    facts about the world of mathematics......
        the characters recorded in literature......
            the phenomena of nature......
                facts and events of history......
                      the beauty of music and art, and
                          the wonders of the mystery of God......

As you sit in the quiet of who you are......
    think about several of your favorite activities or
        projects of the school year......

    What was it you liked about the activity or project?......
                                    ......

    What did you learn from the activity or project?......
                                  ......

    Who are the new friends you met this year?......
                              ......

    What new insight about God
        will you take with you as you complete this school year?......

Have you experienced in a new way, or at a deeper level
> the fact that no matter what is happening,
> > God is present
> > > to help and guide you?......
> > > > ......

Thank you, God, for being present within me.
> Thank you for your help and guidance......

Thank you for the fun I have had,
> for the many things I have learned
> > the things I have learned about myself
> > > and all I have learned about the world you have made......

As you sit in the quiet of God's presence
> remember the first day of the school year......

> the day you stood in the doorway of your new room
> > looking around at the newly cleaned room,
> > > the newly waxed floor,
> > > > the sparkle of new books and
> > > > > the excitement you felt as you began
> > > > > > a new year......

> Remember the day you blessed your teacher,
> > > > and your classmates......

> The day you blessed the school secretary
> > *(name the school secretary)*, who would
> > > take care of all the papers you would take to the office......

> the librarian *(name the librarian)*,
> > who would help you each time you went to the library......

Remember the first day of school when
> you blessed the people who would keep the building clean......

Optional - - - - - - -

> > and you blessed the cooks.
> - - - - - - -

> Remember that first day when you were excited
> > about all the new experiences
> > you would have during the year......

Well, all of that has happened

      the school year is about to end
           and you are waiting to begin your summer vacation......

You are waiting to be free,
      free to sleep longer in the morning......
           to play more......to go on vacation......
                  and to read books just for fun......

As you prepare to begin summer vacation,
      give thanks for the year you are completing......
                  ......

      In the quiet of your heart
           give thanks to God for all you have received......

Give thanks for your favorite activity or project......

      your new friends......

           all you have learned......

And give thanks for God's help and guidance......
                  ......
                  ......

Spend some time alone with God
      asking for a safe and enjoyable summer......
                  ......
                ......

God of love, I thank you for all you have given me,
      for all I have learned,
           and for your presence.

God of creation, I thank you for the gift of summer,
      for the sun and the rain,
           for warmth and for growing things,
                  I thank you for the opportunity to enjoy your creation.

God of all, I ask that you watch over me and guide me,
      I ask that you keep my friends in your care and
           I ask your blessing on myself and others,
                I ask this in the name of Jesus......
                          Amen......
                          ......
                          ......

When you are ready, open your eyes.

Close this meditation with one of the suggested exercises found on page 8.

Playing and Praying with Creation

Stewards of the Earth

Begin this meditation with the opening exercise found on pages 7 and 8.

As you sit quietly in God's presence......
    imagine you are sitting on top of the world......

As you look around you see the vast oceans......
    You see the various landforms......
        the different continents......
            the mountains and valleys,
    You see rooftops......
        straw huts......
            makeshift tents......
                adobe houses and skyscrapers......

    You see herds of elephants......and rhinoceros......
        antelope and elk......
            birds of every color and every size......

    You see rivers and streams......
        rock formations and glaciers......

    You see vast areas of grass and desert lands......
        forest preserves and meadows......

    You see people riding in cars and buses while others walk......
        people in a hurry and people sitting under shade trees......
                                   ......

As you look around and you smile, reverently enjoying God's creation......
    As you sit quietly you remember the places you have been,
        the marvels you have seen......
                ......
                    ......

Thank you God for all of creation!......

Enjoying the fruits of God's creation
> you continue to look, seeing more with each glance……

You become aware of the sun as it shines,
> giving light and warmth……
>> You become aware of a gentle breeze on your face……
>>> the coolness of the earth on which you sit……

As you look closer
> you see giant clouds of smoke coming from very large buildings……

You see pockets of air that seem heavy with smog……
> You see trash lining the shores of the rivers and ponds……
> You see hillsides where trees have been ripped out……

You see acre upon acre of ground
> where trash and garbage have been piled up……
>> You see cars and trucks
>>> forming lines that go on for miles and miles……

You become aware that you haven't seen some animals you used to see……
> You haven't seen any bald eagles……
>> or white rhinoceros……
>>> You've seen only a few white spotted owls……
>>>> and even fewer pandas……

You wonder what is happening……
>> ……
>> ……

You remember hearing reports on the news
> of the air quality index that says stay indoors if at all possible……
>> smog counts that exceed healthy levels……

> the river quality index that makes it dangerous to swim……
>> or to go boating……
>> ……
>> ……

In zoos you find signs that give information
> about animals that are in danger of becoming extinct……

You remember reading articles
> in the newspapers or magazines about strip mining……

You listen to the news and know that this industry or that industry
> is dumping harmful waste in our waterways……

You learn that technology
      continues to make more and more demands on power plants......

What is happening?
      What are we doing?
            you ask yourself......
                ......

The Earth given as gift by God is irreverently being destroyed......
                         ......
                            ......

What is my part in helping to make things better?......
      What is my part in helping to make God's creation
                    viable for the future?......

What small thing can I do, once a day......
            once a month......
                that would say,
                    I reverence God's creation!......
                         ......
                           ......

God of infinite love,
      you make all things......

God of infinite love,
      you make all things new!......

    God of infinite love,
        you have given me life and love
            and the use of all that is created in your name......

In loving response to all that is,
     give me the insight and courage to reverence the earth,
        caring for all life, knowing that all is given to me
           not for my use alone, yet given to my generation
              to nurture and to care for,
                  handing it on to generations to come......
                           ......
                            ......

When you are ready, open your eyes.

Close this meditation with one of the suggested exercises found on page 8.

The Air We Breathe

Begin this meditation with the opening exercise found on pages 7 and 8.

As you sit quietly in God's presence close your eyes......
    Sitting with your eyes closed, listen carefully......
        As you listen God begins speaking......
            ......
                ......

"I want you to remember that I created the earth
    and all living things for your enjoyment......

"The air is for you to breathe......
    the water to quench your thirst, to refresh you
        and to keep you clean......
            the light to illumine the world......
                and the sun to keep you warm
                    and to help the plants to grow......

"All I have created is for you and all living things......

    The air you breathe is the air Abraham and Sarah breathed......

        The air you breathe is the air
            my son Jesus and his mother Mary breathed......

"Your own daughters, sons, your grandchildren,
    and all people after them will breathe the air you breathe......
        You must protect it and keep it clean for their use"......

Trees and all green plants help in keeping the air clean......
    Trees and all green plants use the sun and carbon dioxide from the air
        to make their own food, and in so doing
        they put a clean supply of oxygen into the air
            for you to breathe......

The trees and the green plants
    are having a hard time keeping up with the demands
        that people are putting on the air......

Imagine for a minute a very hot summer day......
    a day when the air we breathe looks cloudy,
        a day when the air looks like smoke......

This happens when people do not take care of the air......
    This happens when people think the air is just for them
        and they don't need to help protect it for generations to come......

This happens:
    when people in factories pollute the air with all kinds of waste......
        when people travel alone each day as they go to work......
            or when all kinds of chemicals are allowed
                to evaporate into the air......
Air was created for you to breathe......
    The air was created so butterflies and birds could fly around
        and find food,
           and build nests and lay eggs......

Air was created to carry bubbles and balloons, and for airplanes......

Air was created to blow through your hair......
    and to blow upon your face......

Air was created so the leaves could dance......
    and snowflakes could be carried to the ground......

Air was created for life and love and beauty......
    Air was created to be reverenced and to be cared for for all time......

For a while think about the air you breathe......
    Think about the cloudy air you have seen......
        Think about how the air gets to be like smoke......
                ......

Now give yourself a little time to think about ways
    you can help to protect the air......
        ......

    How can you help?......
        What can you do to cut down on the pollution in the air?......
                ......
                ......

As you think about the air you breathe,
    Thank God for the gift of creation......
        Thank God for the green plants that keep giving us clean air
            to breathe......

The leader of prayer may wish to say a prayer as the meditation ends, rather than have the children give thanks in a quiet prayer.

When you are ready, open your eyes.

Close the meditation with one of the suggested exercises found on page 8.

Soil

Begin this meditation with the opening exercise found on pages 7 and 8.

Sitting in God's presence, take yourself for a walk......
    Go to the woods......
        the mountains......
            a farm......
                a ball field......
                    or perhaps your own backyard......

Wherever you go, walk around for a while......
    See everything there is to see......

Tell yourself everything you see......
    Call everything by its name......
        leaf......twig......grass......a piece of paper......dandelion......
            butterfly......pine needles......an old tire......an empty can......
        ants......rows of corn......a caterpillar......
            a rock......a flower......a bumblebee......
                ......

Keep looking to make sure you see all there is to see......
            ......

Isn't it beautiful
    as the sun shines through the trees
        adding color and brilliance to each act of creation?......

Stoop down and take some soil into your hands......
    Look at the color of the soil......
        See the rich browns......and the reds......
            ......
    Feel the texture of the soil......
        Is it fine like sand?......Is it lumpy?......
            Is it one big hunk of dirt?......
                What is the texture of the soil?......
                    ......

What is the temperature of the soil you hold?
   Does it feel warm?......
      Is it cool to the touch?......

The soil you hold is created by God......
   created to enhance the earth......
      created for the plants and trees......
         created as the womb of all vegetation......
                              ......

In your heart and in your mind
   thank God for the soil of creation!......
                  ......
                  ......

For a while think about all you have seen......
   the grass......rocks......flowers......and ants......
      the leaves......a dandelion......a butterfly......
                        ......

      Remember the soil as it passed through your hands,
         its color......its texture......its temperature......

As you do this, you are reminded of news reports
   you have recently heard and seen......

   reports of pesticides being used to kill insects......

   reports telling of the effects of the pesticides
         not only on the land......
            but the long-term effects from their use
               on the people working the fields......

You may not know anyone
   who has been affected by the pesticides......

   You may, however, have seen pictures on the news,
      pictures of people working all day in the fields
                           for very little pay......

You are not sure what all of this means......
   You sense that it is not good......

   not good for the people involved......
      not good for the soil that holds the plants......
         not good for Mother Earth......
                  ......

Mother Earth......
    Our Gift of Creation......

Mother Earth......
    Gift to be shared and nurtured by our generation......
        nurtured for the next generation......
As you sit quietly in your backyard......
    in the woods......
        in the mountains......
            in a field of corn......
                or at the ball field......

Remember the touch of the soil as it passed through your hands......
    remember its color......
        its texture......
            its temperature......

Remember that the soil you touch is an act of creation......
    an act of creation that is
        the womb of all vegetation......
            ......

Thank you, God, for the gift of your creation......
        ......

When you are ready, open your eyes.

Close this meditation with one of the suggested exercises found on page 8.

Gift of Creation: Water

Begin this meditation with the opening exercise found on pages 7 and 8.

Sitting in God's presence, relaxed from the day's busyness,
    let go of your thoughts,
        let your imagination guide your mind......

Imagine for a while that it is raining......

Listen to the sound of rain as it falls on the roof......
        ......

    Be aware of the fresh smell of rain in the air......
        ......

The smell of rain......
    a smell that signals relief on a hot muggy day......
        a smell that may rekindle thoughts of fresh spring growth......
        a smell that perhaps reminds you
            of a day you sat on your porch
                listening to the rain
                      while reading a good book......
                          ......

As you become more and more aware of the rain
                  dancing on your rooftop......
    think about all the ways you enjoy the use of water......
        a tall glass of ice water on a hot day......
            a pool filled with water inviting you in for a swim......
                water that gives you lemonade or kool-aid......

    Water that cooks your potatoes......
        water that washes your apple or orange......

    Water that runs over your body as you shower......
        that washes your clothes and dishes......

    Water that runs in the gutters
        or the drainage ditch during and after a good rain......

Water that baptizes,
      washing you clean, bringing you into God's family......

Water that fills the oceans and seas......
      ponds and puddles......

Water that parted,
      leading the Israelites through the Red Sea
            to freedom from Egyptian slavery......

Water that runs down your face
      when you cry or when you laugh until you cry......

Water that brings new life......
      offering new growth to the many forms of vegetation......

Water, God's gift, our joy......

Water, God's gift, can be a source of destruction
      swelling rivers to overflowing......
            bringing floods and hurricanes,
                  washing away homes,
                        and rich farm land......

Water, God's gift, our friend......
      soothing, renewing, cleansing, healing......

Water, God's gift, is our healer......
      soothing our wounds......
            renewing our tissues......
                cleansing our organs......
                    healing our bodies......

Water, God's gift of creation......
      gift to be treasured......
            gift to be reverenced......

      gift to be blessed and shared......
            gift to be embraced and nurtured......

Water, God's gift......
      gift for all time......
            ......
            ......

As you sit and listen to the rain gently fall on the rooftop
      give thanks for the many ways you use and appreciate water......

God of Creation, we thank you for the gift of water,
        gift that is friend,
              gift that heals......
                      gift that gives life!......
                              ......
                              ......

When you are ready, open your eyes.

Close this meditation with one of the suggested exercises found on page 8.

Gift of Creation: Water

Begin this meditation with the opening exercise found on pages 7 and 8.

Sitting in God's presence,
    let your imagination take you for a walk in the rain......

As you leave your house to go outside
    you take with you a very colorful umbrella......
        Describe for yourself what your umbrella looks like......
            color, size, length and shape of its handle......

Just before walking out the door you kick off your shoes......

The day is warm......
    a light rain is falling......
        you stop for a minute before leaving your porch......

    What are your thoughts as you stand barefoot, umbrella in hand,
        ready to walk in the rain?......
            Listen to what your mind is saying to you......
                      ......
                      ......

After a short time you open your umbrella and begin your walk......
    As you walk, listen to the sound of the rain on your umbrella......
            ......

Listen as the rain bounces on the leaves of the trees......
        Listen as the rain falls on the pavement......
            ......

Be aware of the feel of the rain on your feet......
    How does it feel?......
        Is it cool?......warm?......Does it tickle your toes?......
                ......

As you walk down the street
    rest the rod of your umbrella on your shoulder......
        begin twisting the handle......

As you twist the handle you begin to feel the rain on your face......
    you have tilted the umbrella so
        that it no longer is covering your face......

The rain begins to dance around on your face......
        ......

Be aware of how the dancing rain feels as it falls on your face......
        ......

Enjoying your walk, be sure to let yourself attend to the rain
    bouncing on your umbrella......
        dancing on your face......
            and splashing on your feet......
                ......
                ......

As you reach the corner
    you meet a character you have never seen before......
        a different looking kind of character......
            you stop and look......trying not to stare......

The creature senses your presence and turns to talk with you......
    "Good day," comes the greeting......
    "Good day," you respond......

"Enjoying your walk?"......"Yes," you reply.

"Did you know the rain that is falling upon you
    is filled with many impurities?......

"Why, there is enough acid in this rain to eat your skin......
    There are enough strange gases in the rain
            to harm your lungs......

"The impurities in the air and in the rain mount day by day
    secretly finding their way into your body
        through the gentle falling rain......

"Some of these same impurities are in your drinking water......
    your bath water......
        in your swimming pool......
    in your rivers, and lakes......
            and in the puddles where you stand......
                ......

"Acid rain......
      gases......
           impurities from factories......
                are all polluting the air and the rain
                    making it harmful to you......

"All the water of creation is being contaminated......
    God's gift to you and to all living things is being destroyed......

"Whenever people think something is present for their use
    they seem to take it for granted......
        they use it any way they wish, in any quantity they see fit......
                        ......

"Your people need to stop and think......
    Your people need to know
        that the things given them are to be cared for......
            They need to be reverenced......
                They need to be nurtured......
                ......

"Your people need to know that the water they drink today......
    the water they watch bounce and dance as gentle rain......
        the water in the rivers and lakes and even the puddles......

    is the water their offspring for generation after generation
        will drink, and watch as rain bouncing and dancing
            as the rain you enjoy today bounces and dances
                on your umbrella, on your face and on your feet......
                        ......

"Your people need to learn to care for
        and nurture the water so that people in the future
            will have water to enjoy......

    "Your people need to learn to care for the gifts of creation
        so people in the future
            can care for and enjoy the gifts of creation."......
                ......
                ......

As you stand listening
    and thinking about the things the creature has just said to you
        you sense you are standing alone......
            ......

As you look around
    you see that the creature is gone......

    the creature has disappeared......
        you stand alone in the puddle of rain
            umbrella in hand, feet bare......

the rain gently bouncing and dancing on your umbrella......
    and on your face......
        the rain tickling your toes......
            ......
            ......

When you are ready, open your eyes.

Close this meditation with one of the suggested exercises found on page 8.